ISAAC ASIMOV'S
Library of the Universe

Venus:
A
Shrouded
Mystery

by Isaac Asimov

Gareth Stevens Publishing
Milwaukee

Library of Congress Cataloging-in-Publication Data

Asimov, Isaac, 1920-
   Venus : a shrouded mystery / by Isaac Asimov.
      p.   cm. — (Isaac Asimov's library of the universe)
   Includes bibliographical references.
   Summary: Describes the characteristics of the planet Venus and how
   we discovered them.
   ISBN 1-55532-365-0
   1. Venus (Planet)—Juvenile literature. [1. Venus (Planet)] I. Title. II.
   Series: Asimov, Isaac, 1920- Library of the universe.
   QB621.A83   1990
   523.4'2—dc20   89-43135

A Gareth Stevens Children's Books edition

Edited, designed, and produced by
Gareth Stevens, Inc.
RiverCenter Building, Suite 201
1555 North RiverCenter Drive
Milwaukee, Wisconsin 53212, USA

**For a free color catalog describing Gareth Stevens' list of
high-quality children's books, call 1-800-341-3569 (USA) or
1-800-461-9120 (Canada).**

Cover art © Mark Maxwell

Project editor: Mark Sachner
Editor: John D. Rateliff
Series design: Laurie Shock
Book design: Kate Kriege
Picture editor: Matthew Groshek
Technical advisers and consulting editors: Julian Baum and Francis Reddy

Printed in the United States of America

1 2 3 4 5 6 7 8 9 96 95 94 93 92 91 90

CONTENTS

Nowadays, we have seen all the known planets up close except for distant Pluto. We have seen dead volcanoes on Mars and live ones on Io, one of Jupiter's moons. We have studied Triton, the moon of far-off Neptune. We have detected strange objects no one knew anything about till recently: quasars, pulsars, black holes. We have studied stars not only by light, but by other kinds of radiation: infrared, ultraviolet, x-rays, radio waves. We have even detected tiny particles called neutrinos that are given off by the stars.

The nearest of all the planets, Venus, has remained a mystery for a long time. It has such a thick layer of clouds that for years astronomers could see nothing of its surface. They couldn't tell how quickly it rotated or even if it rotated at all. In this book, we will tell you how much we have now learned about this mysterious planet.

Isaac Asimov

Morning Star, Evening Star

Venus is the brightest of all the stars and planets in the sky. Only the Sun and the Moon are brighter. Unlike most planets, Venus never gets far away from the Sun in the sky, and so it can only be seen just before sunrise or just after sunset. When it is to the east of the Sun, Venus shines in the evening sky like a jewel and is called the Evening Star. When west of the Sun, it shines before dawn as the Morning Star.

The ancients thought the Morning Star and the Evening Star were two different objects. They even gave them different names before they noticed that these two "stars" could never be seen in the sky at the same time. Today we know that they are <u>one</u> object, not two.

Because of its lovely brightness, that object was named after the beautiful goddess of love, Venus.

Opposite: The Moon and Venus team up to form a spectacular duo in this multiple-exposure photograph of Tulsa, Oklahoma.

Right: Venus, the Roman goddess of love.

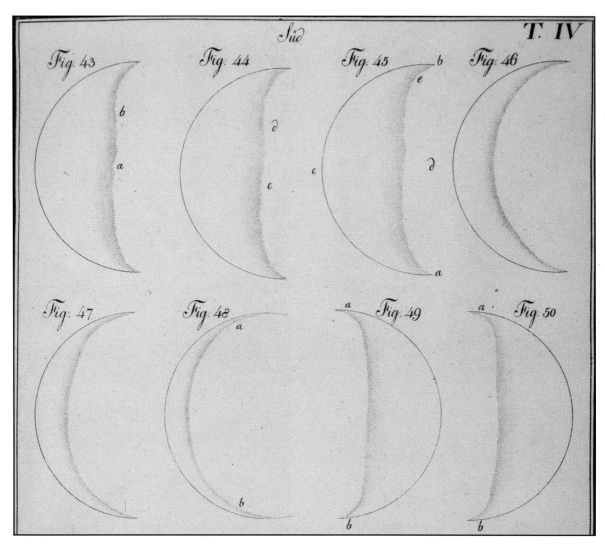

The phases of Venus as recorded by astronomers in the 18th century (above) and the 20th century (below).

Studying Venus

The ancient Babylonians noticed Venus's motion in the sky and became interested in the motions of the other planets, too. This encouraged the growth of astronomy, and of mathematics as well. Ptolemy (pronounced TOL-em-ee), an ancient Greek astronomer, worked out a way of predicting where Venus and the other planets would be at any given time. The only thing wrong was that he pictured Earth at the center of our Solar system, with the Sun and other planets revolving around it.

Italian astronomer Galileo Galilei was the first to use a telescope to view objects in the sky. In 1610, he studied Venus and found that it had phases, like Earth's Moon. Sometimes it was full, sometimes half-lit, sometimes just a crescent. By the old theory that everything went around Earth, Venus should have looked the same all the time. The fact that it changed helped prove that the planets, including Earth, went around the Sun.

Venus — one devil of a planet

The ancient Romans called the Morning Star Lucifer, *which means "bringer of light," for when the Morning Star rose, the Sun would follow. The king of Babylon was also called "the Morning Star." When the king was defeated in battle, the prophet Isaiah said, "How art thou fallen from heaven, O Lucifer, son of the morning!" Centuries later, people thought Isaiah was talking about the devil, cast out of heaven by God, so* Lucifer *became one of the names of Satan.*

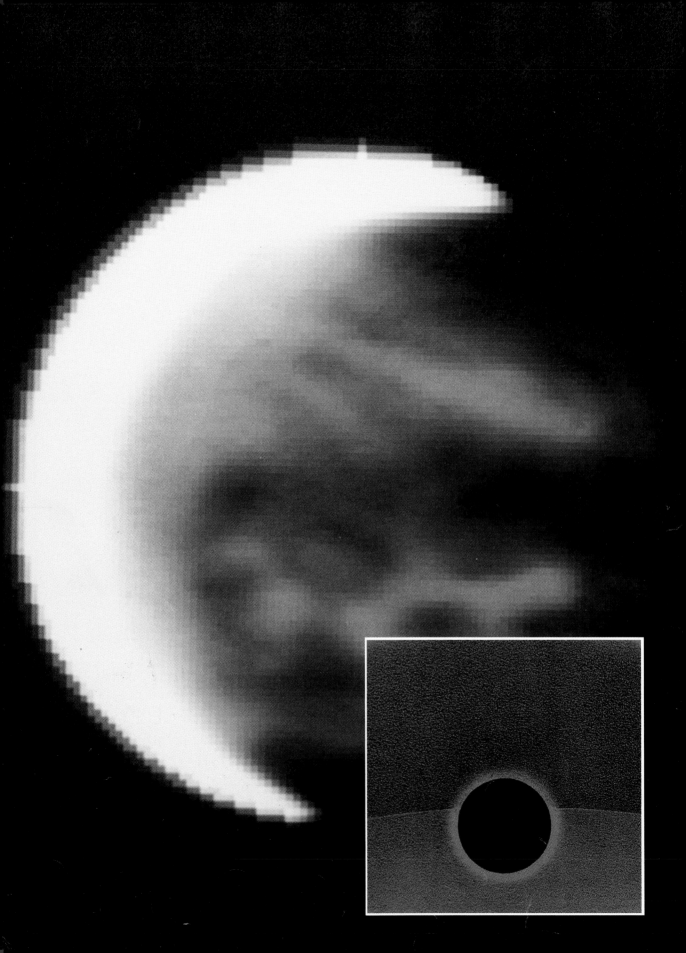

An Ocean of Clouds

When Venus is on the same side of the Sun as we are, it can be as close to Earth as 23.7 million miles (38.1 million km). This is closer than any other large object except for our own Moon. In 1761, a rare event called a solar transit occurred when Venus moved across the disk, or face, of the Sun. By watching this transit of Venus across the disk of the Sun, astronomers could tell that Venus had an atmosphere that contained clouds.

Venus's brightness
— now you see it . . .

As Galileo discovered, what we can see of Venus changes as it moves in its orbit. Our Moon is at its brightest when it's full. But when Venus is full it's on the far side of the Sun and so it's harder to see. When Venus is nearest to us it appears to us as a thin crescent and usually gets lost in the twilight. The best time to view Venus is between these phases, when it looks like a thick crescent.

When we view Venus through a telescope, all we see are its yellowy clouds. For many years this thick cloud cover kept astronomers from learning much at all about Venus's surface — even though it is the planet closest to Earth.

Opposite (background): Heat-sensitive cameras reveal both the sunlit side of Venus (white) and warm clouds on the planet's night side (orange). Below and opposite (inset): The transit of Venus (black circle) in 1874 gave astronomers a chance to examine the planet's thick, cloudy atmosphere.

Venus — A Sister Planet?

The fact that Venus has such a thick layer of clouds made many people think it must have a lot of water on its surface. Venus is closer to the Sun than Earth is. While this means Venus gets more heat than we do, scientists thought Venus's clouds might reflect sunlight and keep the surface from getting too hot.

Some scientists, and many science fiction writers, pictured Mars as an old planet, looking like Earth might in the distant future. They also thought of Venus as a young planet, and imagined that it looked a lot like Earth in the prehistoric past, in the age of the dinosaurs. They pictured Venus as a tropical world with warm oceans and lots of plant and animal life. Since Venus is about the same size as Earth, many people looked upon it as Earth's twin.

In this artist's rendition, a distant volcano blasts a plume of dust and rock high above Venus's Asteria Regio region.

Venus wins the all-around prize!

The planets orbit the Sun in ellipses, which are nearly but not quite circles. Pluto's orbit is so lopsided that there is a difference of 1.4 <u>billion</u> miles (2.25 billion km) between its nearest and farthest distances to the Sun. Earth's orbit is much more regular, with a difference of only about 3 million miles (4.8 million km). But it is Venus, with a difference of less than a million miles (1.6 million km), that has the orbit which is nearest to a perfect circle.

Left: Venus, so unlike Earth in many ways, is close in size to Earth — only about 5 percent smaller than our planet.

Below: Some pictured Venus as a swampy world much like prehistoric Earth.

The Temperature of Venus — Too Hot to Handle

In the 1950s astronomers began studying other kinds of radiation besides the tiny waves we see as light. All objects give off radiation — x-rays, radio waves, ultraviolet, infrared, and light. We can't see most radiation, but we can detect it with the right instruments. What's more, objects that are different temperatures give off different kinds of radiation. So by measuring what kind of radiation an object gives off and how much, astronomers can tell how hot it is.

In 1956, radio astronomers detected the radiation given off by Venus. They showed that Venus must be very hot — hotter than boiling water. Astronomers then knew that the cloud tops were hot. But they still couldn't tell what the temperature on the surface of the planet might be like.

Opposite: a cutaway view of Venus, showing how scientists believe the planet is put together. Like Earth, Venus probably has a hot core of liquid metal.

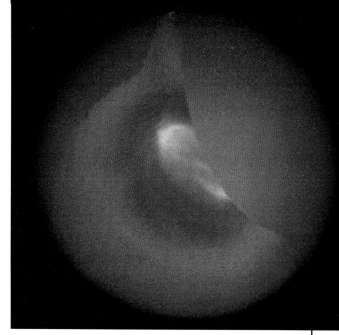

Above: A heat-sensitive camera aboard the Pioneer Venus probe shows the clouds above the north pole of Venus. A dense, crescent-shaped cloud bank spirals outward 10 miles (16 km) above the main cloud deck. The bright spots are probably caused by rapidly moving clouds clearing away to expose the warm atmospheric layers below.

Below: Radio telescopes helped scientists take the temperature of Venus.

In this artist's concept, a Soviet Venera probe stands bathed in an eerie orange light on the surface of Venus.

A Nice Place to Visit, But . . .

There was only one way to find out more about Venus — go there. In 1961, the Soviet Union sent the first of 15 Venera probes to Venus. In 1967, Venera 4 actually descended into Venus's atmosphere and sent back information to Earth. In 1970, Venera 7 became the first probe to send back data from the planet's surface. Mariner 2, the first US probe to study the planet, flew past Venus in 1962. Its instruments showed that the surface of Venus was hot — about 890°F (477°C), hot enough to melt lead!

Venus's intense heat and incredible atmospheric pressure put the Venera probes out of action — but not before they sent back a wealth of information. We now know that Venus's atmosphere is so thick that standing on the planet would feel like being at the bottom of an ocean. We also know that the atmosphere of Venus is made up almost entirely of carbon dioxide, with no oxygen. The lightning-filled clouds also contain water mixed with sulfuric acid.

Background: An artist imagines lightning flashing in an orange Venusian sky.
Below: The surface of Venus as photographed by Venera 13. The view includes the bottom of the lander.

Earth's Twin or a Case of Mistaken Identity?

The probes all showed one thing — Venus is <u>not</u> a twin sister of Earth. Except for its size, it is completely different. Venus is far too hot to have oceans of water or any form of Earth-like life. Its surface is completely dry and desolate.

Venus's atmosphere is also completely unlike Earth's — in fact, it is almost the exact opposite. Venus's air is made up of 98 percent carbon dioxide and a little nitrogen. Earth's air is made up of 78 percent nitrogen, 21 percent oxygen, and less than 0.1 percent carbon dioxide.

The weather on Venus is strange by Earth's standards. Only one-sixth as much daylight gets through the clouds as we get here on Earth, so the light on Venus's surface is always dim. The pressure of Venus's atmosphere is 88 times that of Earth's. There is constant lightning up in the clouds. Acid rain falls from the sky but never reaches the ground. The blistering heat evaporates the drops before they land.

Opposite: an artist's rendering of hot gases jetting through a vent near one of Venus's volcanoes. Inset: Earth's serene beauty is unmatched anywhere in the Solar system — and certainly not on Venus!

Below: Venus as seen when nearest Earth.

Venus, the planet of 584 days — so what's in a number?

Venus moves around the Sun more quickly than Earth does. Every 584 days, Venus gains a lap on Earth. Also every 584 days, Venus is as close to Earth as it can get. Finally, Venus's rotation period is such that every 584 days it turns the same face to Earth. Surely that can't all be just coincidence. Some astronomers think Earth's gravity pulls at Venus and locks it into place. But Earth's gravity seems too weak for that. Could there be some other explanation?

1
Venus Day =
243
Earth Days

The Backwards Planet?

Mariner 2 discovered other surprises about Venus as well. By sending radio waves through the clouds to the surface and then recording the echoes, the probe discovered that Venus rotates very slowly. It takes Venus 243 <u>days</u> to make one turn on its axis, while Earth takes just 24 <u>hours</u>.

What's more, Venus rotates in a direction exactly opposite that of Earth. Earth and most of the other planets turn counterclockwise, from west to east, but Venus turns clockwise, from east to west.

Right: In 1951, R. M. Baum, an English astronomer observing Venus without the benefit of radio astronomy, determined the rotation of Venus to be 195 days.

Opposite (background): In this artist's concept, Mariner 2 determines Venus's rotation by bouncing radio waves off the planet's surface.

Opposite (inset): A more familiar version of the same procedure. At the rate of only one turn on its axis every 243 days, the planet Venus is not likely to receive a rotational speeding ticket!

Famous astronomer E. C. Pickering estimated that Venus took only 21 hours to spin once on its axis.

Lost?
A compass won't help you here!

Venus, Mercury, and Earth all have cores made up mostly of molten iron. As the planet turns, the iron swirls, setting up a magnetic field. That is why Earth is a magnet and why compasses work. But our planet has to turn rapidly to make the liquid center swirl sufficiently. Venus has no magnetic field, so it must turn too slowly. But Mercury turns nearly as slowly as Venus and _does_ have a magnetic field. Why Mercury and not Venus? It's a mystery.

The Mapmaker Probes

When radio waves bounce off an object, they are deflected, or turned aside, by features on the object's surface. By studying the deflections, we can tell what the object looks like, even when we can't see it.

In 1978, a US probe called Pioneer Venus was put into orbit around Venus. Using its radar, it made a map of the entire planet. Radar from the Venera probes has also helped astronomers get a fuller picture of Venus's surface. Venus has no oceans, and only a few craters, so it is not like either Earth or the Moon.

Opposite: Since 1978, the US Pioneer Orbiter has studied the planet's atmosphere and mapped its surface using radar beams.

Below: Several continent-sized regions are evident on radar maps of Venus. The largest, Aphrodite Terra (lower), is about half the size of Africa. The north polar area (circle at top) remains unmapped.

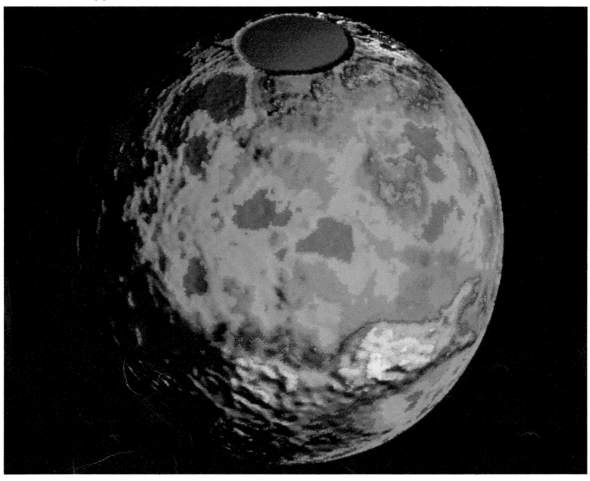

The Map of Venus

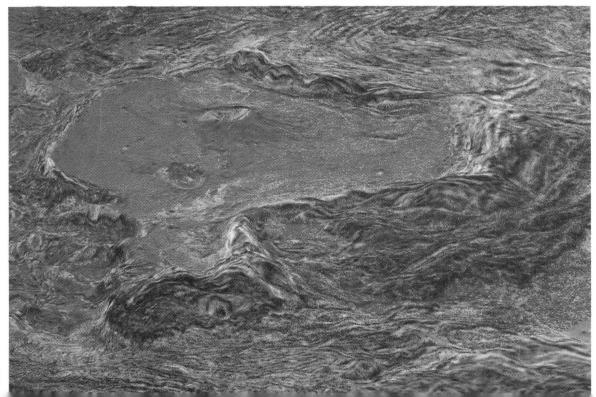

Venus is mostly flat. Earth's surface is made up of pieces called "plates" that slowly move, carrying the continents with them. Sometimes two plates come together and form mountains, like the Himalayas, or cause earthquakes, as in California. But from what we can tell so far, Venus's surface is all one single piece.

Above: Combining data from several sources, including US and Soviet Venus probes, scientists have created this view of the Ishtar Terra region (yellow, near center). The lighter the color, the higher the altitude. Below: Maxwell Montes (orange), the highest mountains on Venus, tower above the flat Lakshmi Planum (purple) area.

There are two areas on Venus that are higher than the rest of the surface, almost like continents on Earth. They contain mountains, some of them higher than any on Earth, and canyons, and what look like extinct volcanoes.

The larger "continent" in the north is called Ishtar Terra, after the Babylonian goddess of love. It is about the size of the United States. The smaller one, named Aphrodite Terra, after the Greek goddess of love, is near the equator. All features on Venus are given women's names, by an agreement of the International Astronomical Union (IAU). This is the group that decides on the names for everything astronomers find in space.

The US Magellan space probe starts its journey from the payload bay of the space shuttle Atlantis. Magellan is designed to provide high-quality radar images of Venus.

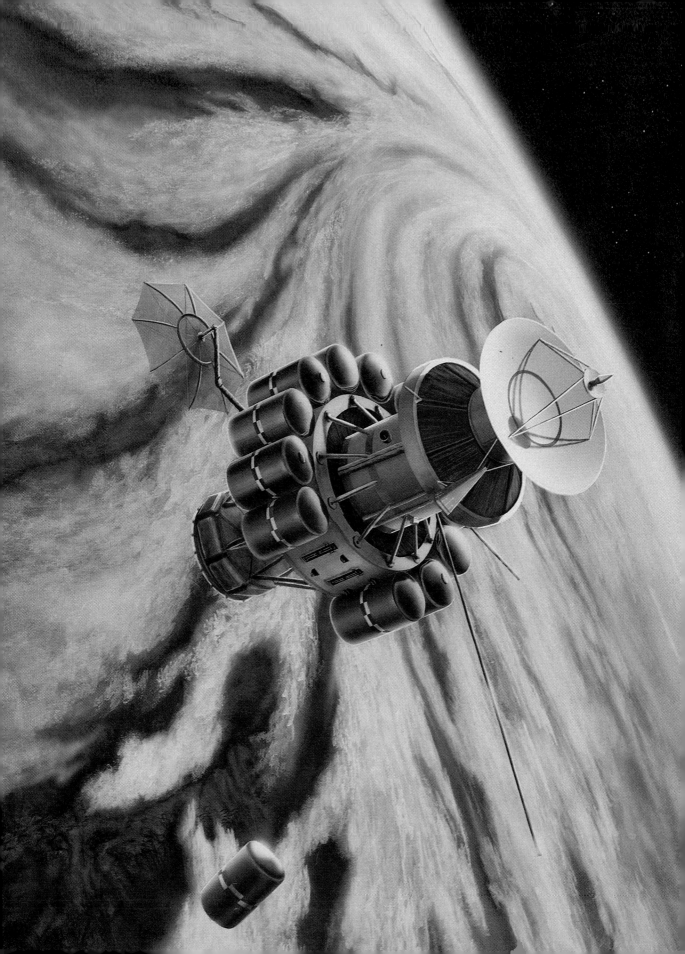

Urban Renewal, Venus Style

Venus is so close to Earth, and so nearly the same size, that it seems quite likely the two planets were similar when they first came into existence. But they developed very differently.

Venus may once have had oceans, like Earth, although we have no way of telling whether they lasted long enough for life to begin. There are still traces of water on Venus today, in the clouds in the form of water vapor.

Some people think that one day we will be able to transform other planets to make them more Earth-like. This is called terraforming. If the clouds on Venus were seeded with plant cells, they might start changing the carbon dioxide into oxygen. This would cause the planet to cool down and become livable. Perhaps some day we will try this experiment.

Opposite: an artist's concept of the seeding of Venus's upper atmosphere. The heavy concentration of carbon dioxide has begun to thin out.

Below: an artist's rendering of the Ashen Light, for hundreds of years one of Venus's most fascinating mysteries.

The Ashen Light — fact or figment?

For centuries, observers looking at a crescent Venus have sometimes been able to see the dark part of its disk dimly lit with a faint rusty brown glow. No one knows what causes this. Could it be auroras or lightning on Venus, or reflected light from our own planet? Some astronomers don't believe it exists at all. If it's an optical illusion, no one can explain what it is. So for now, it remains one of Venus's most baffling mysteries.

?

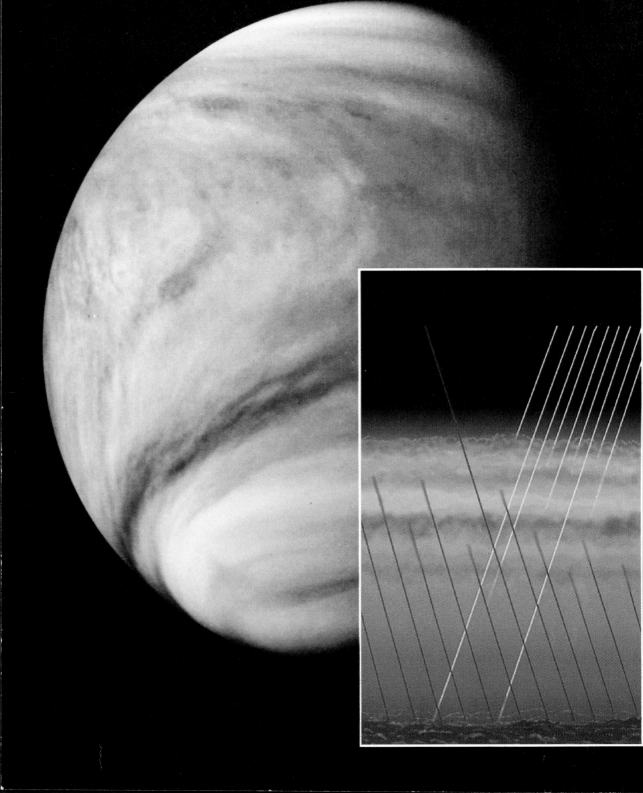

The Greenhouse Effect — What Went Wrong?

If Venus was like Earth to begin with, why did it change? Because Venus is nearer to the Sun than Earth is, it was always warmer. More of its oceans would have evaporated, putting more water vapor in the atmosphere. Water vapor helps hold more of the Sun's heat. This is called the greenhouse effect.

Venus would have gotten still warmer, producing still more water vapor. Carbon dioxide dissolved into the ocean would have begun to bubble out as the water grew steadily hotter. Carbon dioxide in the air also holds onto the Sun's heat, speeding up the process. The temperature would continue to rise until the oceans began to boil — a runaway greenhouse effect. Finally there would be no oceans left, and the temperature would become like that of the inside of a furnace.

We can't be sure that this is what happened on Venus. Whatever happened, Earth has been lucky, at least for now. But some people are afraid that our polluted air will raise the level of carbon dioxide and will cause the same thing to happen here someday.

In a greenhouse on Earth (below), glass walls admit the warming rays of sunlight but keep infrared radiation (heat) from leaving. Something similar happens in Venus's cloudy atmosphere. Opposite (inset): Sunlight (white lines) falls on Venus, but gases in the atmosphere keep heat (red lines) from escaping.

Fact File: Venus

Venus is the sixth largest known planet in our Solar system. The second closest planet to the Sun, Venus never gets very far away from the Sun in our sky. That is why Venus can only be seen just before the Sun rises in the morning or just after it sets at night. Throughout human history, Venus has been known as the Morning Star during its appearance before dawn, and the Evening Star in its appearance after dusk.

Although tiny Mercury is nearer the Sun than Venus is, it is too small and too close to the Sun to be easily spotted from Earth. Venus, on the other hand, is not only clearly visible from Earth, but it is the brightest of all the planets and stars in the sky. Only the Sun and Earth's Moon are brighter. In fact, there have been reports of Venus's "shining" brightly enough on a moonless night to cast shadows on Earth!

We know much more about Venus today than we did only a few decades ago. Since the 1960s, Soviet and US probes have been studying Venus, its atmosphere, and its thick layer of clouds. It is these clouds that obscure Venus's surface, give the planet its bright appearance, and hold in the intense heat of the Sun. Thanks to the probes, Venus is no longer thought of as Earth's mysterious "twin." Yet it remains one of the most beautiful and intriguing objects to grace our sky.

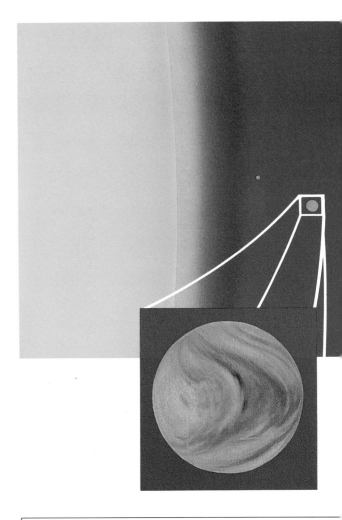

Venus: How It Measures Up to Earth

Planet	Diameter	Rotation Period
Venus	7,521 miles (12,101 km)	243 days*
Earth	7,926 miles (12,753 km)	23 hours, 56 minu

The Sun and Its Family of Planets

Above: the Sun and its Solar system family, left to right: Mercury, Venus, Earth, Mars, Jupiter, Saturn, Uranus, Neptune, and Pluto.
Left: Here is a close-up of Venus. Thanks to the probes sent to explore Venus, we know more about the intensely hostile conditions lurking beneath — and within — the cloud cover of this lovely planet.

Period of Orbit Around Sun (length of year)	Known Moons	Surface Gravity	Distance from Sun (nearest-farthest)	Least Time It Takes for Light to Travel to Earth
4 days, 14 hours	None	0.88**	66.8-67.7 million miles (107.4-108.9 million km)	2 minutes, 6 seconds
5 days, 6 hours	1	1.00**	91.4-94.5 million miles (147-152 million km)	—

* Venus rotates, or spins on its axis, once every 243 days. But its retrograde (opposite-direction) rotation and the time it takes to orbit the Sun make a Venusian "day" — sunrise to sunrise — 117 Earth days long.
** Multiply your weight by this number to find out how much you would weigh on this planet.

More Books About Venus

Here are more books that contain information about Venus. If you are interested in them, check your library or bookstore.

Journey to the Planets. Lauber (Crown)
Mars and the Inner Planets. Vogt (Franklin Watts)
On the Path of Venus: Discovering the Structure of Our Solar System. Motz (Pantheon)
Our Solar System. Asimov (Gareth Stevens)
The Solar System. (National Geographic)
Venus, Near Neighbor of the Sun. Asimov (Lothrop, Lee & Shepard)

Places to Visit

You can explore Venus and other parts of the Universe without leaving Earth. Here are some museums and centers where you can find many different kinds of space exhibits.

Reuben H. Fleet Space Theater and
    Science Center
San Diego, California

Dow Planetarium
Montreal, Quebec

Doran Planetarium
Sudbury, Ontario

Sudekum Planetarium
Cumberland Science Museum
Nashville, Tennessee

Yerkes Observatory
Williams Bay, Wisconsin

Burke-Gaffney Planetarium
Saint Mary's University
Halifax, Nova Scotia

Fernbank Science Center
Atlanta, Georgia

Albert Einstein Planetarium
National Air and Space Museum
Washington, DC

For More Information About Venus

Here are some people you can write to for more information about Venus. Be sure to tell them exactly what you want to know about. And include your full name and address so they can write back to you.

For information about Venus:
National Space Society
922 Pennsylvania Avenue SE
Washington, DC 20003

The Planetary Society
65 North Catalina
Pasadena, California 91106

About missions to Venus:
NASA Jet Propulsion Laboratory
4800 Oak Grove Drive
Pasadena, California 91109

Stardate
McDonald Observatory
Austin, Texas 78712

Space Communications Branch
Ministry of State for Science and Technology
240 Sparks Street, C. D. Howe Building
Ottawa, Ontario K1A 1A1 Canada

Glossary

Aphrodite Terra: one of the two "continents" on Venus, named for Aphrodite, the ancient Greek goddess of love. (See also *Ishtar Terra*.)

atmosphere: the layer of gases that surround a planet, star, or moon. The atmosphere of Venus is very dense, poisonous, and filled with lightning.

billion: in North America — and in this book — the number represented by 1 followed by nine zeroes: 1,000,000,000. In some places, such as the United Kingdom (Britain), this number is called "a thousand million." In these places, one billion would then be represented by 1 followed by *12* zeroes: 1,000,000,000,000 — a million million, a number known as a trillion in North America.

carbon dioxide: a gas (chemical formula CO_2) necessary for plant life. It is a colorless, heavy gas. Carbon dioxide is what gives soda its fizz, and when humans and other animals breathe, they exhale carbon dioxide.

ellipse: an oval; the oval-shaped orbit a planet takes around the Sun.

Evening Star: the name by which Venus has long been known when it appears in the evening sky after sunset.

Galileo Galilei: the Italian astronomer who in 1610 studied Venus through the first astronomical telescope.

"greenhouse effect": the phenomenon whereby heat entering a planet's atmosphere becomes trapped and continues to build up until the surface temperature of the planet is raised. It is thought to be responsible for Venus's being the hottest known place in the Solar system other than the Sun.

infrared radiation: "beneath the red" radiation. Infrared wavelengths are longer than red light wavelengths. Infrared radiation is invisible to the naked eye, but you can feel it as heat.

Ishtar Terra: the northernmost of Venus's two "continents," about the same size as the United States, named for the Babylonian goddess of love. All planetary features on Venus have female names. (See also *Aphrodite Terra*.)

Lucifer: a Latin name meaning "bringer of light," applied both to Venus as the Morning Star (because it rises before the Sun) and to the devil (as the most glorious of angels before his fall).

magnetic field: the force that surrounds a planet like an "atmosphere" of energy. Earth's magnetic field allows compasses to work. Venus, alone of all the planets we have explored, has no detectable magnetic field.

Morning Star: the name by which Venus has long been known when it appears in the morning sky before sunrise.

solar transit: the passing of a planet or other smaller astronomical body across the disk, or face, of the Sun.

sulfuric acid: a corrosive liquid able to dissolve solid rock. It is found in Venus's atmosphere, making Venus one place where there is truly "acid rain."

Venus: the ancient Roman goddess of love. The planet was named after her because of its great beauty.

Index

The publishers wish to thank the following for permission to reproduce copyright material: front cover, © Mark Maxwell, 1986; p. 4, photograph by William P. Sterne, Jr., Tulsa, Oklahoma; p. 5, © Keith Ward, 1990; pp. 6-7 (lower), photographs courtesy of New Mexico State University Observatory; p. 8 (full page), photograph courtesy of Crisp, Sinton, Ragent, Hodapp, 1989; pp. 8 (inset), 9, observations of the transit of Venus, 9 December, 1874, from the collection of Yerkes Observatory; pp. 10, 14-15 (background), 16 (full page), © MariLynn Flynn, 1987; pp. 11 (upper, both), 13 (upper), 23, 26 (full page), courtesy of NASA; p. 11 (lower), © MariLynn Flynn, 1990; p. 12, © Paul Dimare, 1990; p. 13 (lower), photograph courtesy of the Naval Research Laboratory; p. 14 (inset, upper), © David Hardy; pp. 14-15 (inset, lower), © Sovfoto; p. 16 (inset), © Matthew Groshek, 1980; p. 17, © Julian Baum, 1990; p. 18 (full page), © Garret Moore, 1990; p. 18 (inset), © Rick Karpinski/DeWalt and Associates, 1990; p. 19 (upper), from the collection of the Yerkes Observatory; p. 19 (lower), courtesy of Richard Baum; p. 20, illustration courtesy of NASA; p. 21, Jet Propulsion Laboratory; p. 22 (both), courtesy of the United States Geological Survey; p. 24, © Mark Maxwell, 1990; p. 25, © Richard Baum, 1990; p. 26 (inset), © Garret Moore, 1989; p. 27, courtesy of Mitchell Park Conservatory; p. 28 (inset), © Thomas O. Miller/Studio "X"; pp. 28-29 (upper spread), © Sally J. Bensusen.